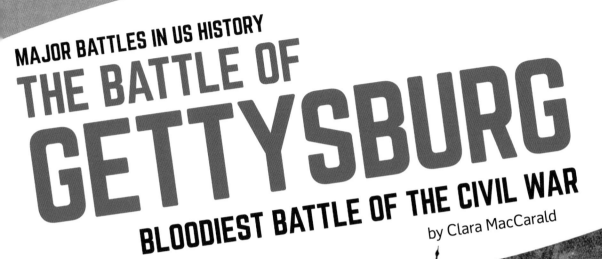

Major Battles in US History

THE BATTLE OF GETTYSBURG

BLOODIEST BATTLE OF THE CIVIL WAR

by Clara MacCarald

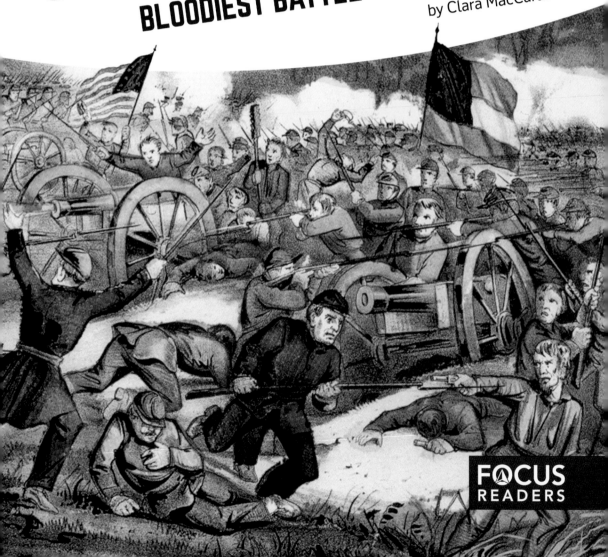

FOCUS READERS

WWW.NORTHSTAREDITIONS.COM

Produced for North Star Editions by Red Line Editorial.

Photographs ©: Currier & Ives/Library of Congress, cover, 1; Red Line Editorial, 5; Library of Congress, 6–7; Map by Hal Jespersen/www.cwmaps.com, 9, 21; Gary Ombler/Dorling Kindersley/DK Images, 10 (left); Chris Pondy/Alamy, 10 (bottom right); Sementer/Shutterstock Images, 10 (top right); Everett Historical/Shutterstock Images, 12–13, 22; Kurz & Allison/Library of Congress, 15; Timothy H. O'Sullivan/Library of Congress, 17; North Wind Picture Archive, 18–19; Hulton Archive/Archive Photos/Getty Images, 25; Michael Poe/iStockphoto, 26–27; Library of Congress/AP Images, 29

Content Consultant: Erik B. Alexander, PhD, Assistant Professor of History, Southern Illinois University Edwardsville

ISBN
978-1-63517-018-4 (hardcover)
978-1-63517-074-0 (paperback)
978-1-63517-178-5 (ebook pdf)
978-1-63517-128-0 (hosted ebook)

Library of Congress Control Number: 2016949828

Printed in the United States of America
Mankato, MN
November, 2016

ABOUT THE AUTHOR

Clara MacCarald is a freelance writer with a master's degree in biology. She writes educational books for children. She has also written about news and science for local publications in central New York.

TABLE OF CONTENTS

November 6, 1860: Abraham Lincoln is elected president of the United States.

December 20, 1860: South Carolina becomes the first Southern state to leave the Union.

April 12, 1861: The Confederate States of America start the US Civil War by firing on Fort Sumter.

June 3, 1863: Confederate general Robert E. Lee sends his army north to invade the Union.

July 1, 1863: Union troops retreat to the high ground south of Gettysburg, Pennsylvania, on the first day of the battle of Gettysburg.

July 2, 1863: Lee's army attacks the Union line, which holds.

July 3, 1863: The battle of Gettysburg ends with a Union victory after the failure of Pickett's Charge, a Confederate assault focused on the Union center.

July 4, 1863: The Confederate army retreats back to the South.

April 9, 1865: Lee surrenders to Union general Ulysses S. Grant, ending the Civil War.

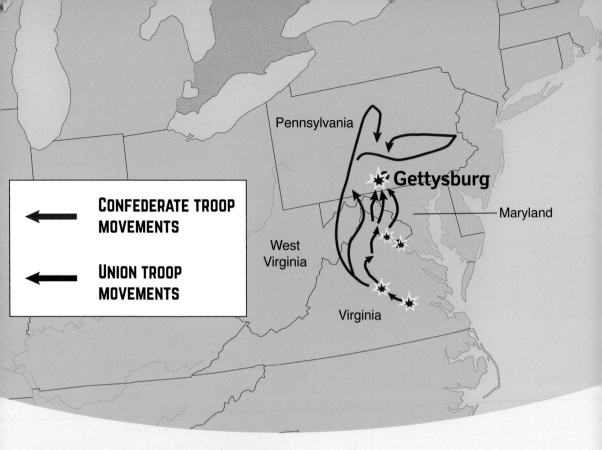

Pennsylvania

Gettysburg

Maryland

West
Virginia

Virginia

←	**CONFEDERATE TROOP MOVEMENTS**
←	**UNION TROOP MOVEMENTS**

BATTLE OF GETTYSBURG

	UNION ARMY	CONFEDERATE ARMY
Killed	3,155	2,592
Wounded	14,529	12,700
Captured or Missing	5,365	4,150

CHAPTER 1

RETREAT THROUGH TOWN

Confederate colonel Abner Perrin called his soldiers to a stop. It was July 1, 1863. Fields littered with dead and wounded soldiers stretched out behind Perrin's **brigade**. Ahead lay the town of Gettysburg, Pennsylvania. Fights between Union and Confederate troops had roared around Gettysburg all day.

Fighting broke out in the fields surrounding Gettysburg on July 1, 1863.

Perrin's brigade had recently arrived at the battle and was awaiting orders. In the distance, other Confederates pushed forward, driving Union forces back into Gettysburg. In response, the Union **artillery** blazed to life from the outskirts of town. The Confederates took cover near the **barricade** that stretched along the edge of the town.

Major General William Pender ordered Perrin to move forward to help overtake the Union troops in Gettysburg. As Perrin and his men marched ahead, they passed exhausted Confederate soldiers.

Perrin's brigade waded across a stream and lined up on the other side. Here they planned their attack. Perrin told his men not to fire their weapons. Instead of shooting, they were to fight up close with their **bayonets**.

GETTYSBURG: DAY 1

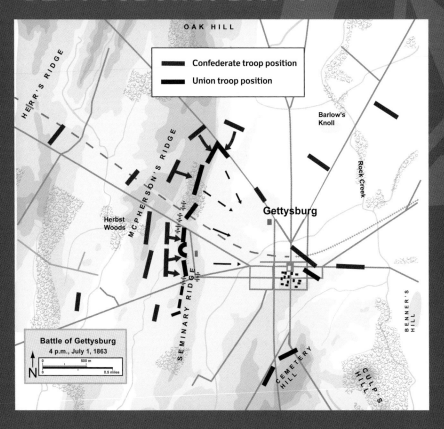

OAK HILL

Confederate troop position

Union troop position

HERR'S RIDGE

Barlow's Knoll

Rock Creek

MCPHERSON'S RIDGE

Herbst Woods

Gettysburg

SEMINARY RIDGE

BENNER'S HILL

Battle of Gettysburg
4 p.m., July 1, 1863

N

500 m

0.5 miles

CEMETERY HILL

CULP'S HILL

Perrin's brigade ran toward the wall sheltering Union troops. Artillery shells rained down. Rifle blasts mowed down the attackers. Some Confederates retreated.

THE SPRINGFIELD RIFLE

Many soldiers at Gettysburg shot Springfield rifles. To arm the gun, a soldier rammed powder and a single minié ball, or bullet, into the barrel.

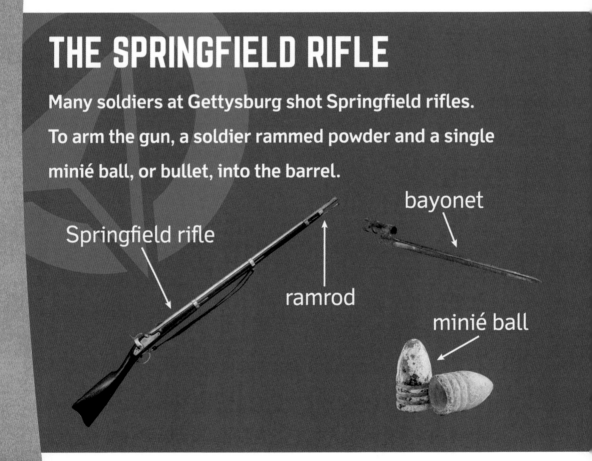

Springfield rifle

ramrod

bayonet

minié ball

Perrin's brigade slipped around the barricade. Union soldiers retreated and disappeared into Gettysburg. Perrin's soldiers rushed into buildings to capture the hiding Union soldiers. Soon, Perrin's soldiers raised the Confederate flag over the town square.

The Union had lost the town. And it seemed the Union had also lost the battle. But from town, the Confederates could see Union troops gathered on the high ground to the south. The Union army was preparing for another fight. This battle would last another two days. The bloodiest battle of the Civil War (1861–1865) had just begun.

CHAPTER 2

THE SOUTH INVADES THE NORTH

By the time fighting broke out around Gettysburg in July 1863, the Civil War had raged for more than two years. But tension between the US government and Southern states had been growing for even longer.

In November 1860, Americans elected Abraham Lincoln as US president.

Abraham Lincoln was strongly against the spread of slavery in the United States.

However, many citizens in Southern states did not want Lincoln to be president. Lincoln wanted to outlaw slavery in new US territories. Southerners tended to think the people in the territories should decide whether to allow slavery. As a result, Southern states began to leave the United States, or Union. They formed the Confederate States of America. Then, in April 1861, Confederate artillery attacked Fort Sumter, a Union fort. The Civil War began.

At first, the war was fought in the South. Then, in 1862, Confederate general Robert E. Lee invaded the North. He hoped a big win on Union soil could

The battle of Antietam ended in a draw, but it successfully sent Lee's army back to the South.

end the war. But Lee's forces were stopped in Maryland at the battle of Antietam, and they returned to Virginia. In 1863, after winning two major battles in the South, Lee tried going north again. Lee's army plunged into Pennsylvania.

The Union army raced to protect Washington, DC, and other major cities. On June 30, 1863, Confederates came across Union soldiers near Gettysburg. Both armies began to move. Lee prepared for battle near a city west of the town. Union major general George Meade planned to defend a position to the south. Union brigadier general John Buford posted his **cavalry** around Gettysburg.

Both armies' plans changed when the conflict began early the next morning. A few miles west of Gettysburg, Buford's soldiers began shooting at Confederate figures in the shadows. The Union cavalry were outnumbered. But they held off

Cemetery Hill provided high ground to the south of Gettysburg.

their opponents until Union **infantry** arrived. A long fight followed. Finally, the Confederates drove the Union soldiers back through Gettysburg. Those who made it through gathered on Cemetery Hill south of town. There the rest of the Union army began to gather.

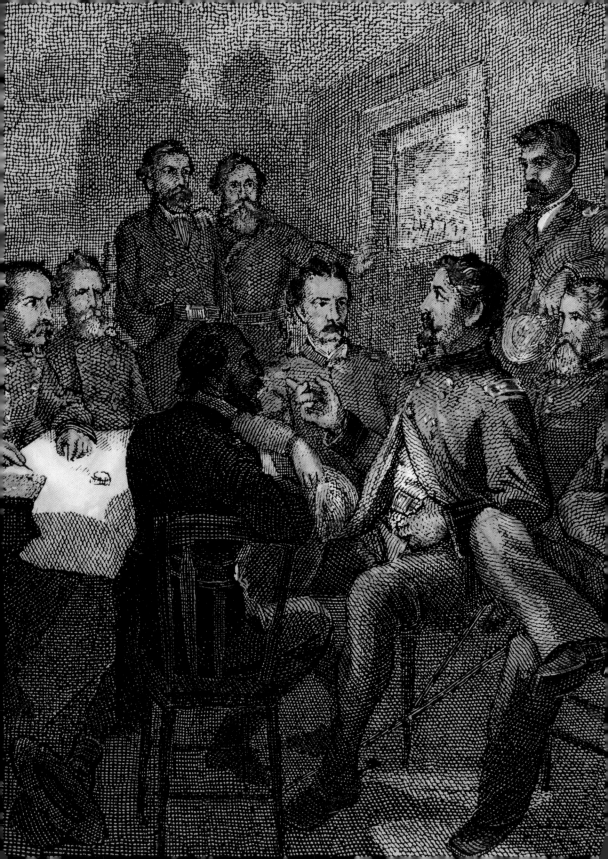

CHAPTER 3

THE UNION STANDS ITS GROUND

Meade arrived at the Union's position after midnight. In a small farmhouse on Cemetery Hill, he decided to take a defensive position. He ordered his soldiers to fan out along the high ground.

The next day, on July 2, Lee told Confederate lieutenant general James Longstreet to strike the Union's left **flank**.

Meade meets with Union officers in a farmhouse on Cemetery Hill to plan.

Other groups would move against different parts of the line. Longstreet's men spent hours marching to find a way to sneak around the Union lines. The day grew late. Longstreet's men moved toward a hill called Little Round Top. Four pieces of Union artillery were waiting for them in a place called Devil's Den. The artillery had been dueling with Confederate cannons all day. Now they fired at Longstreet's infantry, but the cannons shot over the soldiers' heads. Longstreet's men surged into Devil's Den. The Union soldiers fled.

Longstreet's men continued toward Little Round Top. It was the far edge of the Union line. If they broke through, the Confederates could attack the rest of the Union army from behind. Union troops led by Colonel Joshua Chamberlain held the hill and fired at the Confederates.

GETTYSBURG: DAY 2

Battle of Gettysburg
Overview: July 2, 1863

Confederate troop position
Union troop position

GETTYSBURG

Oak Ridge

LEE
Seminary
Seminary Ridge
A. P. HILL
HOWARD
NEWTON
Cemetery Hill
Culp's Hill
Benner's Hill
EWELL
SLOCUM
Spangler's Spring
Wolf's Hill
HANCOCK
MEADE
Power's Hill
SICKLES
SYKES
SEDGWICK
Peach Orchard
Rose Woods
Wheatfield
Devil's Den
Little Round Top
LONGSTREET

N
0   1 km
0   1 mile
450 ft 500 ft 550 ft 600 ft

Union soldiers fire artillery from Little Round Top.

When they ran out of **ammunition**, Chamberlain's soldiers charged with bayonets. Fighting raged until night fell. Confederates took some ground, but the Union line held. Dead and wounded men covered the battlefield.

Meade met with his generals at midnight. They agreed to wait for Lee's attack on July 3 rather than go on the offensive. In the morning, Lee began a massive attack with Longstreet in command. Horses pulled artillery pieces to the Confederate front lines. But many shots flew over the Union's front line. The Union artillery responded but held back to save ammunition. After almost two hours, the thunder of the artillery stopped. Then more than 11,000 Confederate infantry lined up. Major General George Pickett commanded three of the nine brigades. Their attack came to be known as Pickett's Charge.

Pickett's men marched out of the woods 1 mile (1.6 km) from the high ground. As they got closer, they began to run. Shells and bullets tore through their lines. Many Confederates retreated. But some reached the Union lines. Brigadier General Lewis Armistead led men over a stone wall. Union soldiers began to run away. But they soon recovered and fought back. Armistead fell, wounded. So did many others. Some Southerners surrendered. Others fled.

While Pickett's Charge distracted soldiers on the front lines, Confederate cavalry sneaked around the Union line. There they met the Union cavalry.

Pickett's Charge approaches the Union line.

Some members of the Union cavalry carried more advanced rifles called repeaters, which could fire multiple times in a row. The Union cavalry chased off the Confederate cavalry. The remains of Pickett's Charge also retreated. The Southerners had lost the battle.

CHAPTER 4

THE SOUTH RETREATS

The next day, Lee's army began limping home. His hope of a victory to end the war was over. On the other side, Lincoln praised the Union army for the win but also wanted Meade to continue attacking. Another battle might win the war for the Union. But Meade's soldiers were exhausted. No battle occurred.

Lee's soldiers retreat into Virginia across the Potomac River.

Wounded soldiers from both sides crowded into Gettysburg. Villagers and soldiers rushed to bury the dead. A cemetery was created in the town. Lincoln spoke at the **dedication** of the cemetery on November 19. His speech, the Gettysburg Address, gave meaning to the battle. He said the soldiers' sacrifice had made the ground sacred. To honor that sacrifice, Lincoln said the country must not allow the Union to perish.

The fighting dragged on, but never again did Lee try to invade the North. Nearly two years after the battle of Gettysburg, Lee surrendered. Soon after, the war was over.

Former Union and Confederate soldiers shake hands at the 50th anniversary of the battle of Gettysburg.

The year 1913 was the 50th anniversary of the battle. Veterans from both sides met at Gettysburg. They reenacted Pickett's Charge. Fifty years earlier, they had been bitter enemies. Now, on the battlefield, they came together as Americans.

FOCUS ON
THE BATTLE
OF GETTYSBURG

Write your answers on a separate piece of paper.

1. What events led to the battle of Gettysburg?

2. Why do you think Lincoln believed a Union win in the Civil War would honor those who died at Gettysburg?

3. Where did Union leaders gather after the first day of the battle of Gettysburg?

- **A.** Cemetery Hill
- **B.** Devil's Den
- **C.** Little Round Top

4. Which is the most likely reason for Lee wanting to move the fighting onto Union soil?

- **A.** He thought the North's cooler weather would be good for his soldiers.
- **B.** He thought a victory in the North would make the Union want to end the war.
- **C.** He thought he would be able to recruit Northerners to join his army.

Answer key on page 32.

GLOSSARY

ammunition
Objects that are shot from weapons.

artillery
Large mounted guns or cannons.

barricade
A structure that blocks people from moving past.

bayonets
Long knives attached to the ends of rifles.

brigade
A large group of soldiers that is part of an army.

cavalry
A military force with troops who serve on horseback.

dedication
A ceremony to officially complete or open something.

flank
The right or left side of a military line.

infantry
A military force with troops who serve on foot.

TO LEARN MORE

BOOKS

Allen, Thomas B., and Roger MacBride Allen. *Mr. Lincoln's High-Tech War.* Washington, DC: National Geographic, 2009.

Miller, Mirella S. *12 Questions about the Gettysburg Address.* Mankato, MN: 12-Story Library, 2016.

Stanchak, John E. *Civil War.* New York: DK, 2015.

NOTE TO EDUCATORS

Visit **www.focusreaders.com** to find lesson plans, activities, links, and other resources related to this title.

INDEX

Answer Key: 1. Answers will vary; **2.** Answers will vary; **3.** A; **4.** B